SERENDIPITY

Published in Australia by
Bambini Media
Street: 1 Douglas Street, Pascoe Vale, 3044 Australia
Email: delgrosso.cinthia@gmail.com
Website: www.bambinimedia.com

First published in Australia in 2021
Copyright © Cinthia Del Grosso 2021

All rights reserved. No part of this publication may be reproduced, stored in a retrieval system, or transmitted, in any form or by any means without the prior written permission of the publisher, nor be otherwise circulated in any form of binding or cover other than that in which it is published and without a similar condition being imposed on the subsequent purchaser.

National Library of Australia
Cataloguing-in-Publication entry

 A catalogue record for this book is available from the National Library of Australia

ISBN: 978-0-6488877-7-5 (paperback)

Graphic design by Sophie White
Printed by Ingram Spark

Disclaimer: All care has been taken in the preparation of the information herein, but no responsibility can be accepted by the publisher or author for any damages resulting from the misinterpretation of this work.
All contact details given in this book were current at the time of publication, but are subject to change.

Serendipity

*(n) finding something beautiful
without looking for it*

CINTHIA DEL GROSSO

For Mum
with all my love.

When I was a young woman, my mother always encouraged me to write my reflections on the life I was living. Sometimes I would share my poems with friends or family. Before I did, I always shared them with my mother. She would always smile and tear up as I presented her with a new poem.

While most people know me as a mother, sister, colleague, wife or friend, my mother knows me as a human being living her best life. My mother related to the essence of humanity in my poems and encouraged me to publish them. Each poem was written as a reflection of a particular moment in time in my life and each poem has an underpinning story.

The emotions shared are universal—hope, happiness, sadness, fear, etc. It is these shared emotions that make us all human. I hope this small book resonates with you too. I hope it makes you smile and, also, tear up as I share with you my innermost observations and emotions in this little collection of poems.

Cinthia

THE WOMAN IN BLUE

My Nonna had a picture that hung above her bed,
I always loved that picture, so was given it when wed.
A beautiful young mother with a sleeping child abreast,
I'd silently admire it as I lay myself to rest.

A simple prayer I'd pray each night,
To the woman dressed in blue,
Then close my eyes to dream my dreams,
My conscience clear and true.

I hoped one day the time would come,
When as a mother too,
I'd cradle my own sleeping child,
Like the woman dressed in blue.

SOULMATES

The winds of time will pass us by,
But steadfast we will stand,
Souls united through time and space,
Not by the hands of man.

For while our souls will grow and change,
To live this Earthly life,
From time to time they will connect,
Like a husband with his wife.

When our Earthly time has passed,
To the 'soul pool' we will go,
You and I will find each other,
When our souls, once more, will glow.

THE MIGRANTS SONG

I'm going to Australia,
A country far away,
I'm leaving all my family,
To find a better way.

A place to raise my children,
And make myself a home,
But as I board this crowded ship,
I feel so all alone.

My town is in the distance,
My loved ones left behind,
With them all my memories,
Keep flashing through my mind.

The schoolyard of my childhood,
Our noisy street-gang games,
The buildings with their musky smells,
Shops and old street names.

I still see mother's anxious tears,
Streaming down her face;
God grant me strength and courage
To succeed in this new place!

I'll make new friends and family,
A home, a job, a life.
I'll work the long and lonely hours,
And then call for my wife.

Then if one day I go back,
To the town I called my own,
My heart will be divided,
And both places will be home.

SOPHIA FOUND SIX

Sophia was a little girl who liked to count and play.
She liked the number five a lot and found it every day.

She found five fingers and five toes.
She found two eyes, two ears, one nose.

Two hands that clap, two feet that dance.
Two little legs that like to prance.

One mouth that giggles through rosebud lips:
Sophia blew kisses when she found six!

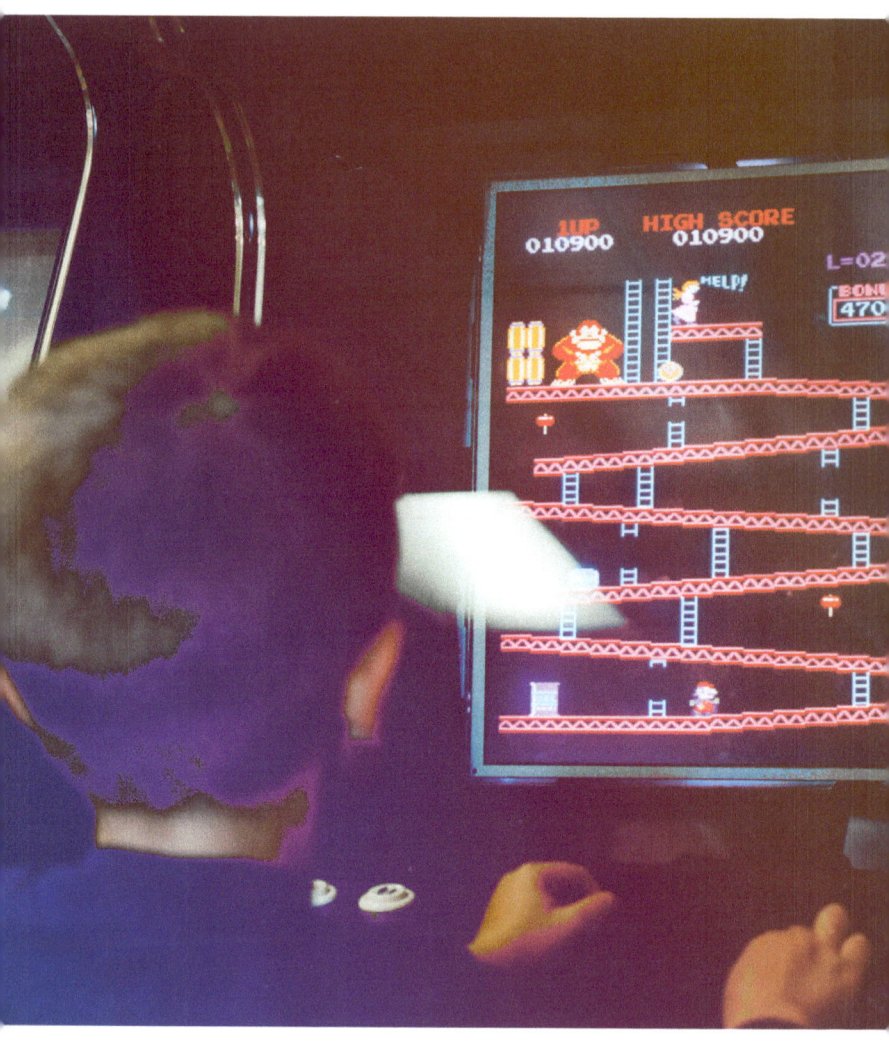

GAME BOYS

Get your game boy, start the game.
Jump and push and score.
Play the game and win the points,
Then start, just as before.

They sit there quietly playing,
Eyes straight-ahead and tense.
For it takes some concentration
And lots of common sense.

And while they are just game boys,
And while it's just a game,
Their minds are getting ready,
For life is much the same.

They'll jump the hurdles,
Gain the points,
Fall,
Then start again,
To stay alive,
And reach stage 5,
When living lives as men.

DAYBREAK

Up at five, yes, still alive!
A lark sings its solo song.
The moon gives way to the break of day,
A train goes rambling along.

A new day starts.
Two birds now sing.
The light invades my home.
The growing noises fill the air;
I know I'm not alone.

A yawn, a stretch,
A chorus of birds,
Hot shower, a coffee and more.
I pack my things while magpies sing,
Then I'm out the door!

FOG

Ten million droplets of water
left hanging in the air.
While now and again some dew drops fall
to remind me they are there

Stillness and silence surround me ...
shattered by a barking dog,
while blindly I keep on walking
through mountain mist
... and fog

MELANCHOLY RAIN

Sadness overwhelms me.
My heart is filled with pain.
My feelings mirrored outside
by the melancholy rain.

Thoughts of days and years gone by,
of long forgotten love,
but all the while memories and rain
keep falling from above.

They tap, tap, tap against my heart
and on the windowpane,
my mind is clouded over
by the melancholy rain.

You told me that you loved me,
and said you'd always be true,
but now you've gone and left me here
and I'm alone and blue.

It tap, tap, taps against my heart,
and on the windowpane.
My pain is mirrored outside
by the melancholy rain.

WAVES

Rolling to the shore,
they just keep on coming,
each one chasing the one before.

When they arrive,
they break up like laughter—
sparkling champagne bubbles on a sandy shore.

Tumbling over each other, they end their long race—
sand warmly greets them, drinks them …
waves fade,

While the wet sand reminds me
of the forces of nature & my soul
feels refreshed,
just by watching the waves.

THE ORDINARY MAN

I met an ordinary man once,
A man much like myself.
I didn't know his name or rank,
Or state of mental health.

Our governments were different,
Had opposing views on rights.
They called on us, the ordinary men,
To go off to war and fight.

He silently approached me.
My reactions were ready on cue,
But when I looked into his tired, sad eyes,
They told a story I knew.

It was the story of a spirit,
Of a father and a son,
The story of an ordinary man,
Now standing with a gun.

We looked into each other's eyes
And seemed to understand,
Though we didn't speak the language
Of this far and foreign land.

A moment passed between us
Though no battle had begun,
Courageously, he turned and walked
While lowering his gun.

The dawn brought with it peacetime,
A new era had begun.
I thanked the Lord for the ordinary man
Who hadn't used his gun.

To the ordinary men of this planet,
My message is but one,
Show strength, courage, and tolerance …
Then the battle will be won!

A PERFECT SPRING DAY

A perfect Spring day, with smiles all around,
basking in the warmth of the love that I found.
I knew one day soon you'd go away,
my soul cried in anguish and begged you to stay.

But the winds of change blew, and so came the time,
when that perfect Spring day was a memory of mine.
I remember that day and the warmth of the sun
and in the depths of my soul know love can't be undone.

I feel in my heart that Spring day was a sign,
that for all eternity, you'll always be mine.
Our love didn't end on that perfect Spring day,
not in March or December, not even in May.

A father's love is as pure as the moon and the sun,
and like the stars in the heavens, we'll always be one.
Always connected, through time and through space,
joined by our love, regardless of place.

As I bask in the sun on this warm Autumn day
I still feel you beside me and silently pray
that God keeps you safe, free of pain and life's trials …
in closing my eyes, I see your warm, loving smile.

MY MOTHER REMEMBERS

My mother remembers her life as a child:
The people and places she saw.
She laughs at the stories of far, foreign places
with loved ones who are no more.

She cries at the thought of the war all around her
and the fear and the hunger she felt.
Then talks of post-war days when things were much better,
though they still had to 'tighten the belt'.

She looks at me kindly and asks if I know her …
and could I come often and stay?
Then drinks her tea quietly, reliving life's memories …

Not knowing who I am today.

THE GARDEN
OF GETHSEMANE

We each have our own garden
of olive trees far away,
a garden we go to
when we face our darkest day —
to still our mind and question
what our life was for,
to beg to be spared a little more time,
to live, just a little bit more.

But the garden has no answers
and its' stillness lingers on,
rich oils of olives remind us
of where we all come from —
we are just one with nature,
we grow; we live; we die,
our death will come when our God decides
our spirit is ready to fly.

THE MIRROR
OF MY LIFE

I looked in the mirror and what did I see?
The face of a child was looking at me,
with blue eyes of innocence and golden blonde hair,
I turned for an instant and she wasn't there.

I looked in the mirror and what did I see?
A sparkling teenager was grinning at me,
with the future before her, and the world at her feet,
the smile seemed to linger as she made her retreat.

I looked in the mirror and what did I see?
Veiled face of a bride was glowing at me.
She cried tears of happiness as all seemed to stare.
She took a deep sigh and then wasn't there.

I looked in the mirror and what did I see?
The eyes of a mother were smiling at me,
a deep sense of joy held in two sets of eyes,
a lifetime of loving and strong family ties.

I looked in the mirror and what did I see?
A middle-aged woman was looking at me,
her face showed the lines of the life she'd worn,
a quieter smile greeted each weary morn.

I looked in the mirror and what did I see?
A very old woman was looking at me,
her hair all white and her skin quite wrinkled,
but oh, when she smiled, her knowing eyes twinkled!

I looked up from my deathbed and what did I see?
The light of my God was shining on me:
"Though you never saw me, you were never alone!"
I knew, at that moment, that I was at home.

SHE MADE A DIFFERENCE

On one day, of one week, in one year,
People gathered together to remember her.
"She made a difference," they all said.

Some remembered her loving embrace.
For others it was her womanly ways:
her smile, her touch, her encouraging words,
her humour, her courage, or her funny moods.

Her meals, her garden, bright laughter, faux pas,
a word of comfort, or a cup of tea ...
she was a gentle lady, who meant the world to me.

Her sighs in the night, so loud and clear,
the pain in her eyes mirrored her fear.
sweet tears down her face ...
that face of grace ...

She made a difference!

FREE AT LAST

There is a place I call my own,
somewhere by the sea.
I watch my family from above
and am me—really me!

Like a bird above the trees
I glide along the gentle breeze,
feel my love blowing in the wind,
now that my spirit's flying free.

So life's a song that you must sing,
a song of love and family,
just hold me always in your heart,
because you are a part of me.

And when you watch the clouds above,
or gaze out at the peaceful sea,
feel my love blowing in the wind
now that my spirit's flying free.

ABOUT THE AUTHOR

Cinthia Del Grosso's books have received wonderful reviews from a range of sources, including The Duchess, Sarah Ferguson, SCBWI (Australia East and New Zealand), and on Goodreads. Cinthia lives in Melbourne, Australia with her husband, and an exceptionally active dog. She helps look after her elderly mother as well as her grandchildren from time to time.

Before she started writing Children's Picture Books, Cinthia held a Diploma of Teaching from Melbourne State College and taught as a Primary School Teacher for several years. After that, just to shake things up, she got a Diploma of Vocational Educational and Training and spent many years writing Vocational Training Strategies for Industry as well as Nationally Recognised Qualifications.

Then, she did a handful of consultancies with some influential people, who are way too dignified to be named here. She ran her own consultancy company for several years before beginning her own Publishing Company—Bambini Media.

From a very young age, she always wrote poetry. Poetry was Cinthia's way of reflecting upon events in her life to help her understand those events and her emotional responses to them.

If you want to know when Cinthia's next book will come out, please visit her website at **http://www.bambinimedia.com**. You can send her an email from the 'Contact Us' page, where you can also sign up to receive an email about her up and coming releases.

www.ingramcontent.com/pod-product-compliance
Lightning Source LLC
Chambersburg PA
CBHW041500010526
44107CB00044B/1521